CPS-Peirce ES

3 24891 9800874 7

W9-AKV-949

DISCARD

Peirce Library Media Center
1423 West Bryn Mawr Avenue
Chicago, Illinois 60660
(773) 534-2440

LIGHTNING
BOLT
BOOKS™

How Do Video Games Work?

L. E. Carmichael

PEIRCE LIBRARY MEDIA CENTER
1423 W. Bryn Mawr Avenue
Chicago, Illinois 60660

Lerner Publications • Minneapolis

Copyright © 2016 by Lerner Publishing Group, Inc.

Content Consultant: John Sartori, Assistant Professor, Electrical and Computer Engineering, University of Minnesota

All rights reserved. International copyright secured. No part of this book may be reproduced, stored in a retrieval system, or transmitted in any form or by any means—electronic, mechanical, photocopying, recording, or otherwise—without the prior written permission of Lerner Publishing Group, Inc., except for the inclusion of brief quotations in an acknowledged review.

Lerner Publications Company
A division of Lerner Publishing Group, Inc.
241 First Avenue North
Minneapolis, MN 55401 USA

For reading levels and more information, look up this title at www.lernerbooks.com.

Library of Congress Cataloging-in-Publication Data

Carmichael, L. E. (Lindsey E.), author.
        How do video games work? / by L. E. Carmichael.
            pages   cm. — (Lightning bolt books. Our digital world)
        Audience: Ages 5-8.
        Audience: K to grade 3.
        Includes bibliographical references and index.
        ISBN 978-1-4677-8079-7 (lb : alk. paper) — ISBN 978-1-4677-8313-2 (pb : alk. paper) —
    ISBN 978-1-4677-8314-9 (EB pdf)
        1. Video games—Juvenile literature. 2. Video games—Design—Juvenile literature. I. Title.
    GV1469.3.C377 2016
    794.8—dc23   2014044101

Manufactured in the United States of America
1 - BP - 7/15/15

Table of Contents

Designing Video Games

People around the world love playing video games. Have you ever wondered how these games work?

People use computers to make video games.

Some games are made by one person. Other games involve huge companies.

Shigeru Miyamoto is a famous game designer. He created the Mario and Zelda games.

Game designers come up with ideas for games. The designer thinks of a goal for the player. The goal may be to defeat a villain.

Designers figure out how the game will work. Will the game be a simple puzzle? Will there be a big world to explore? Game designers answer these questions.

Some games, such as Minecraft, have no definite goals or rules.

Designers decide where the game takes place. It may be in a city, a jungle, or even in the future.

Sports games often take place in virtual versions of real-life stadiums.

Some games let you play as yourself.

Designers create characters. The player can control some characters. Others are friends or enemies. Their actions move the game's story forward.

Writing in Code

Video game consoles are computers. The games themselves are computer programs. This means they are written in computer code. This is a language that computers understand. It tells the computer what to do.

Programmers may use many screens to organize their work.

Programmers are workers who write computer code.

Once the design is done, they write the game's code.

Code controls how the game looks and works. Programmers write code for everything you experience in a game.

In tablet games, code controls what happens when you touch the screen.

Testing games is a fun job, but it is also a lot of work.

Game testers play games before they come out. They do everything in the game that a player might try. They take notes on anything that doesn't work right. Testers work with programmers to fix these problems.

Racing games share similar game engines.

Many games share some code in common. Two different driving games may share code for how cars move in the game world. This code is known as a game engine. Some engines are used in many games. Others are used in only one.

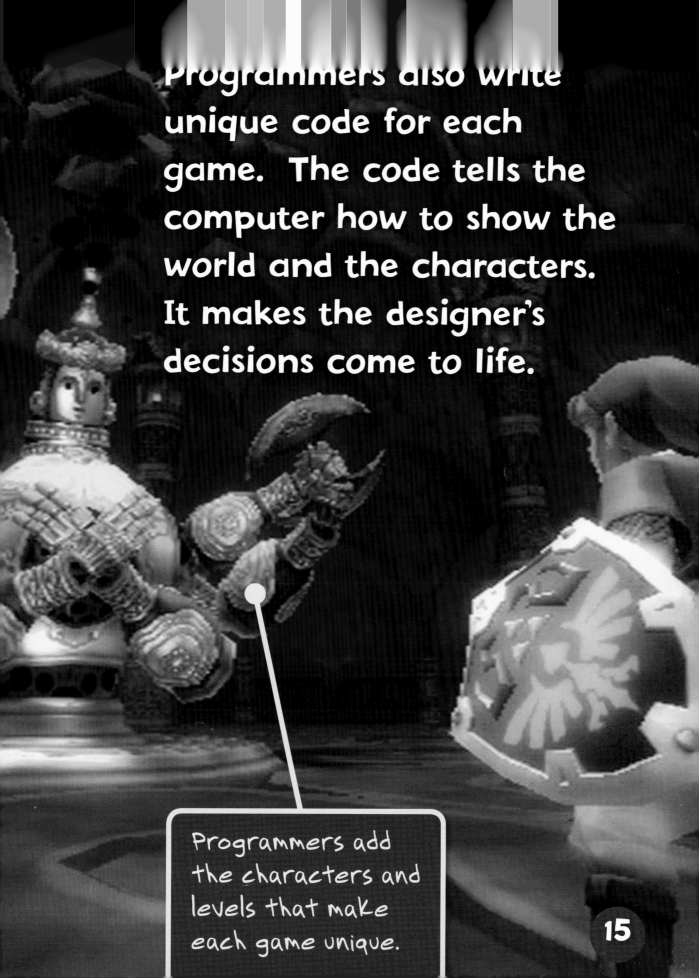

Programmers also write unique code for each game. The code tells the computer how to show the world and the characters. It makes the designer's decisions come to life.

Programmers add the characters and levels that make each game unique.

15

Inside the Console

Code for video games is stored on discs or hard drives. To start a disc game, players put the disc into a console. The console reads the code from the disc.

Most modern games come on discs.

Game consoles also use hard drives to save your progress.

Hard drives are usually found inside game consoles. Games on hard drives don't need discs.

Memory is located on computer chips.

The console copies the code from a disc or a hard drive into its memory. The console can read this memory faster than it can read a disc or a hard drive. Putting code in the memory makes games run faster.

Next, the CPU reads the code from the memory.

The **CPU** is the console's brain. It follows the instructions it reads in the code.

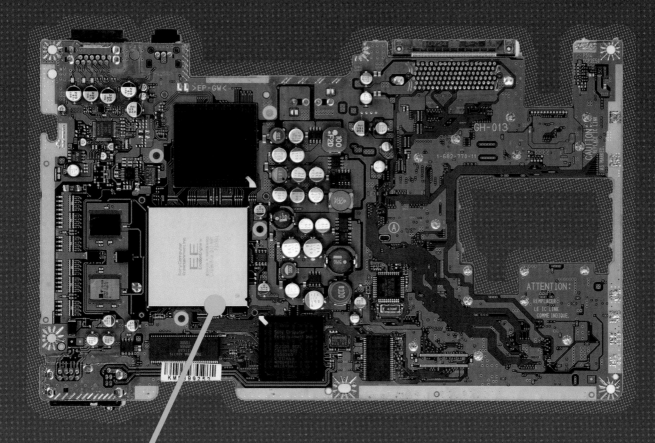

CPU stands for "central processing unit."

Cables carry video and sound from the console to the television.

Parts of the console handle video and sound. The **CPU** tells these parts what to show and what sounds to make. The console sends information to the screen and speakers.

The part that handles video may have its own **CPU** and memory. It works together with the main **CPU** to create the game's graphics.

Handheld consoles have built-in screens and speakers.

Controlling the Fun

Players use controllers to interact with their games. Controllers send signals to the console. Different controllers use different types of signals.

This early game controller had only one button.

Game pads have buttons and joysticks. Pressing a button sends a signal to the CPU. The game code tells the CPU what happens in the game when each button is pressed.

Joysticks control movement. Sensors in the controller measure how far the joystick is being pushed. They send signals to the CPU. The CPU moves the player's character.

Most modern game pads have two joysticks.

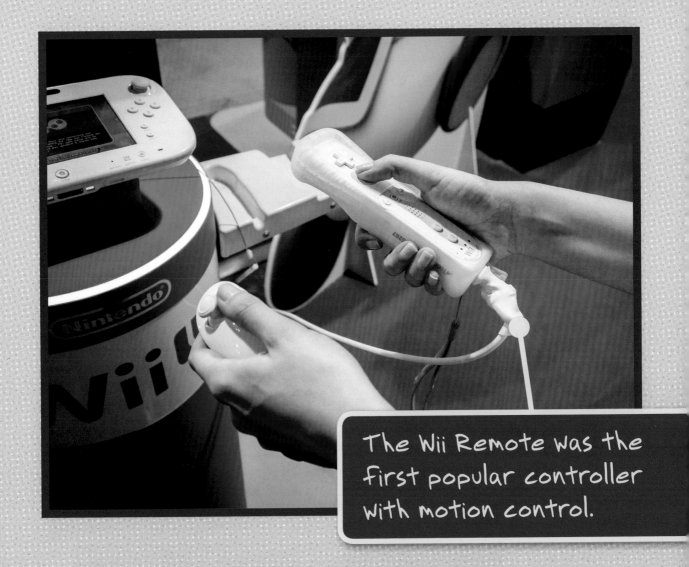

The Wii Remote was the first popular controller with motion control.

The Nintendo **Wii Remote** has sensors that measure the controller's movement. The console can also tell which way the controller is pointing. The **CPU** turns this information into controls in the game.

The Kinect is another way to control games. It does not use a controller at all. Instead, a device shines infrared light into the room. The light bounces off the player's body and reflects back to a camera. Information from the camera tells the CPU how the player is moving.

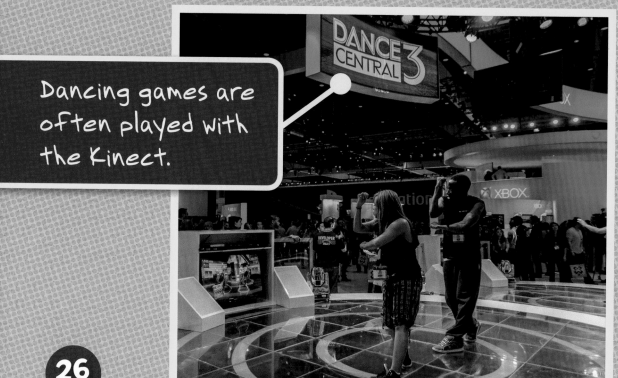

Dancing games are often played with the Kinect.

Takeaway Tips

- Ask an adult to check a game's age rating before you play it. Games rated E are often good choices for kids.

- Different consoles play different games. Before buying a game, make sure it matches your console.

- If you play games online, check with an adult before sharing your name or address.

- Wii Remote and Kinect games are controlled by body movements. Make sure you have enough space to move safely.

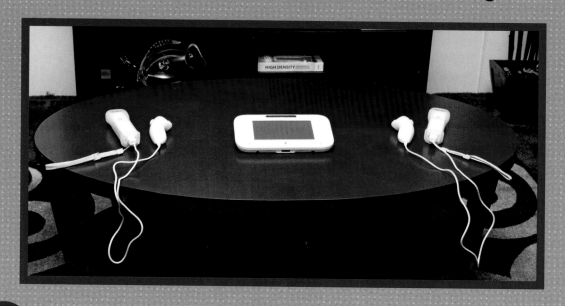

Fun Facts

- Many video games take years to create. Some games are made by teams of more than one hundred people.

- In 1989, Nintendo created the Game Boy. People bought more than one hundred million of these handheld consoles.

- The PlayStation 2 is the top-selling console ever. It sold more than 150 million units.

- By 2014, more than 90 percent of American kids had played video games.

Glossary

console: a computer specially designed to run video games

hard drive: a device used to store information

infrared light: a color of light that cannot be seen by people and is used by some video game systems to sense movement

program: step-by-step instructions that tell a computer how to do something

sensor: a device that measures motion, light, or other physical events

tester: a person who plays video games to find and help fix any errors before the games go on sale

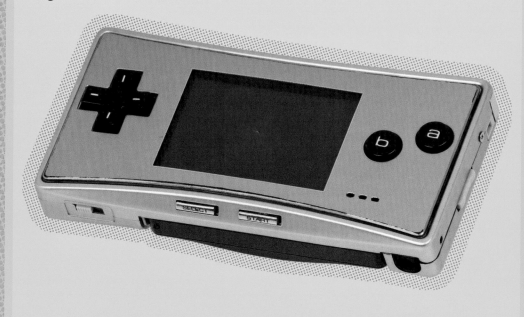

Further Reading

Carson, Mary Kay. *Who Invented Home Video Games? Ralph Baer.* Berkeley Heights, NJ: Enslow Publishers, 2012.

Entertainment Software Rating Board
http://www.esrb.org/index-js.jsp

How Video Game Systems Work
http://electronics.howstuffworks.com/video-game.htm

Pratchett, Rhianna. *Video Games.* New York: Crabtree, 2009.

Suen, Anastasia. *Alternate Reality Game Designer Jane McGonigal.* Minneapolis: Lerner Publications, 2014.

Video Game Revolution
http://www.pbs.org/kcts/videogamerevolution

LERNER 𝓮 SOURCE™

Expand learning beyond the printed book. Download free, complementary educational resources for this book from our website, www.lerneresource.com.

Index

Photo Acknowledgments

The images in this book are used with the permission of: Evan Amos, pp. 2, 10, 17, 18, 19, 21, 23, 24, 30; © Sergey Novikov/Shutterstock Images, p. 4; © Monkey Business Images/Shutterstock Images, p. 5; © Gerard Roussel/Zuma Press/Newscom, p. 6; © Oleg Doroshin/Shutterstock Images, p. 7; © Stefano Tinti/Shutterstock Images, pp. 8, 25; © Ric Francis/AP Images, p. 9; © Jeff Chiu/AP Images, p. 11; © Anatoliy Babiy/iStock Editorial/Thinkstock, p. 12; © Elaine Thompson/AP Images, p. 13; © Photohota/Shutterstock Images, p. 14; © Nintendo/AP Images, p. 15; © ABDesign/iStock Editorial/Thinkstock, p. 16; © Brian Balster/iStock/Thinkstock, p. 20; © tmcphotos/Shutterstock Images, p. 22; © Barone Firenze/Shutterstock Images, pp. 26, 28; © Michael Bowles/Rex Features/AP Images, p. 27; © Lisa F. Young/Shutterstock Images, p. 31.

Front Cover: © wavebreakmedia/Shutterstock.com.

Main body text set in Johann Light 30/36.

Peirce Library Media Center
1423 West Bryn Mawr Avenue
Chicago, Illinois 60660
(773) 534-2440